DK POCKET EYEWITNESS
CATS

FACTS AT YOUR FINGERTIPS

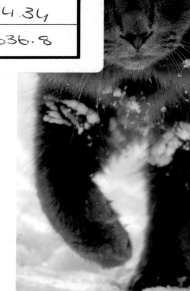

Author Andrea Mills
Consultant Kim Dennis-Bryan PhD, FZS

First published in Great Britain in 2020 by
Dorling Kindersley Limited
80 Strand, London WC2R 0RL

A CIP catalogue record for this book
is available from the British Library.
ISBN: 978-0-2414-1301-2

Printed and bound in China

A WORLD OF IDEAS:
SEE ALL THERE IS TO KNOW

www.dk.com

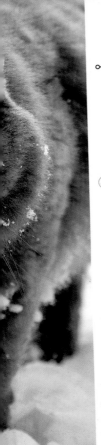

CONTENTS

Ocelot

Conservation status
This book contains information about the conservation status of wild cats:

Endangered – Very high risk of extinction in the wild.

Vulnerable – High risk of extinction in the wild.

Near threatened – Likely to become threatened from extinction in the near future in the wild.

Least concern – Does not yet qualify for any of the above categories in the wild.

Scales and sizes
The profiles of the wild cats in this book have scale drawings to show their size in relation to an average adult male human.

1.8 m
(6 ft)

What is a cat?

Cats are carnivorous (meat-eating) mammals belonging to the Felidae family, which is made up of about 40 species of wild cat and all domestic breeds. Many wild and domestic cats have patterned fur, while others have coats of a single colour. Most wild cats live and hunt alone away from humans, but the domestic breeds are tame and socialize with people.

Feline features

A cat's body and bone arrangement give it the feline features of acute senses, agile movement, and speed. These cat characteristics are shared by both wild species and most domestic varieties.

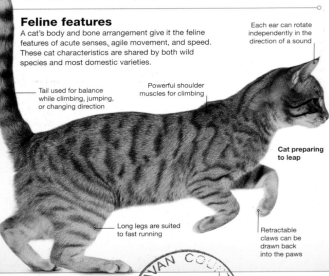

Each ear can rotate independently in the direction of a sound

Tail used for balance while climbing, jumping, or changing direction

Powerful shoulder muscles for climbing

Cat preparing to leap

Long legs are suited to fast running

Retractable claws can be drawn back into the paws

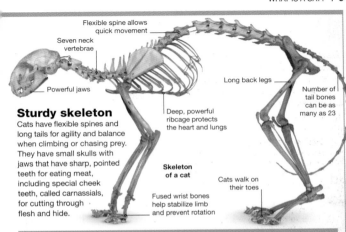

Flexible spine allows quick movement

Seven neck vertebrae

Powerful jaws

Long back legs

Number of tail bones can be as many as 23

Sturdy skeleton

Cats have flexible spines and long tails for agility and balance when climbing or chasing prey. They have small skulls with jaws that have sharp, pointed teeth for eating meat, including special cheek teeth, called carnassials, for cutting through flesh and hide.

Deep, powerful ribcage protects the heart and lungs

Skeleton of a cat

Cats walk on their toes

Fused wrist bones help stabilize limb and prevent rotation

Selection and survival

Wild cats and pedigree domestic cats are both subject to selection. Wild cats roam free and hunt to eat, with only the best-equipped cats surviving in the wild. This natural selection has led to the evolution of today's wild cats. Pedigree cats are subject to artificial selection because humans closely control their breeding.

Tiger, a wild cat

Ragdoll, a pedigree cat

The cat family

All cats belong to the same carnivore family, the Felidae. This family is divided into two groups: the Felinae is made up of small cats and includes the domestic cat, *Felis catus*, while the Pantherinae is a smaller group that contains the seven species of big cat.

FELIDAE

FELINAE

SMALL CAT GROUP	CARACAL GROUP	OCELOT GROUP	BAY CAT GROUP
African wildcat, black-footed cat, Chinese mountain cat, European wildcat, jungle cat, sand cat, and domestic cat	African golden cat, caracal, and serval	Andean mountain cat, Geoffroy's cat, kodkod, margay, ocelot, oncilla, pampas cat, and southern tiger cat	Asian golden cat, bay cat, and marbled cat

Serval

Margay

Marbled cat

African wildcat

Domestic cat

The domestic cat evolved from the African wildcat and lives on every continent except Antarctica.

Prehistoric relative

The earliest feline fossils date back 34 million years. They show that the first cats were often larger and fiercer than today's big cats. The now-extinct sabre-toothed cats shared a common ancestor with modern cats, but today's cats did not evolve from them.

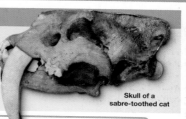

Skull of a sabre-toothed cat

PANTHERINAE

Indochinese clouded leopard, jaguar, leopard, lion, snow leopard, Sunda clouded leopard (also called Diard's clouded leopard), and tiger

LYNX GROUP

Canadian lynx, bobcat, Eurasian lynx, and Iberian lynx

PUMA GROUP

Cheetah, jaguarundi, and puma

LEOPARD CAT GROUP

Fishing cat, flat-headed cat, leopard cat, Pallas's cat, rusty-spotted cat, and Sunda leopard cat

Cheetah

Eurasian lynx

Pallas's cat

Lion

Growing up

Cats are carnivorous creatures and so are adapted for hunting prey and eating flesh. Most are solitary, but it is a different story for newborns. Kittens (or cubs, for the big wild cats) cannot see or hear when they are born, and remain entirely dependent on their mother for the first three months of their lives.

Litter of kittens

A mother cat gives birth to a litter of about 3–5 kittens. They all snuggle up together for warmth and the mother can recognize each of her kittens by their individual scent.

A newborn kitten's eyes are closed and its ears are folded for the first week of its life.

Litter of sleeping kittens

Kittens feeding on
the mother cat's milk

Mother's milk

Kittens start to feed on their mother's milk almost immediately after birth and continue on milk for the first month of their lives. This milk contains all the nutrients the kittens need as well as antibodies – proteins that protect against infection.

Learning skills

Kittens learn how to be effective hunters by pouncing on toys and jumping out at their siblings. Playtime develops quicker reactions, helping kittens learn how to protect themselves in any future fights.

Kitten pouncing
on toy

Cat years

The first two years of a cat's life are a period of rapid growth equivalent to 25 years in a human's life. After this, each cat year is about the same as four human years.

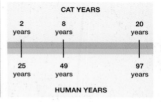

CAT YEARS		
2 years	8 years	20 years
25 years	49 years	97 years
HUMAN YEARS		

Feline forms

Not all domestic cats look the same. They can differ in shape and size, as well as colour and coat length. When combined with differences in their faces, ears, eyes, and tails, it can result in very different-looking cats. Set standards define the desired appearance of each pedigree breed.

Body basics

Cats are immediately recognizable even though breeds that originated in hot climates are slender and athletic, while those from cooler climates tend to be stocky. Exceptions are found in "dwarf" breeds, which have shorter legs, and hybrid cats, which are larger than most breeds.

The Persian has a round, flat face

Face to face

Cat faces can either be round or long and wedge-shaped, or round and flat, which creates striking differences in appearance between breeds.

The Sphynx has a long, wedge-shaped face

Cats have a long back for their size, which gives them flexibility and agility

Unique folded ears tilt forwards on the head

Scottish Fold

All ears

Most cats have upright ears, with either pointed or rounded tips. A notable exception is the Scottish Fold; its ears fold forwards. The American Curl's ears curve back instead.

Bright eyes

The first sign of health in a cat is bright eyes. These can be round or slanted in shape, and can be coloured in various shades of orange, green, or blue. Some breeds have odd-coloured eyes.

Chasing tails

Most cats have long tails, which are used for balancing while climbing, and for communicating with other cats. Some breeds have short tails or no tails at all. This Japanese Bobtail has only a stump for a tail.

Coats and fur

Most cats have short fur to protect their skin. For wild cats, a sandy red solid colour or a coat with spotted or striped patterns camouflages them in their habitats. Domestic cats have many more coat colours and patterns, and can have long or curly fur. Some breeds have been selectively bred to have little fur.

Coat colours and patterns

Cat coats have a bewildering variety of colours and patterns, or a combination of the two, many developed from careful selective breeding and our knowledge of genetics and inheritance. Six of the most common are shown here.

Self: Also known as a solid coat, self is one colour only, including black, white, or blue.

Particolour: This coat features two or more colours in distinct patches.

Tabby: These coats feature darker patterns of swirls, stripes, or spots, on a paler ticked fur.

White spotting: A coat that has patches of white of various sizes is produced by a gene that prevents any colour from developing.

Fur pigmentation

Cat hair has different levels of pigmentation. A self colour comes from an even distribution of colour pigment along the hair shaft. When only the end has colour, the coat is tipped (⅛), shaded (¼), or smoke (½). No pigment at all creates white fur and a hair that alternates with bands of no colour is ticked.

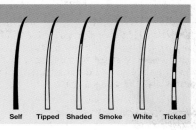

Self   Tipped   Shaded   Smoke   White   Ticked

Pointed: This coat features a light base colour with darker areas on the ears, face, paws, and tail.

Tortie: Short for tortoiseshell, the tortie coat is patterned with colours such as red and black or blue and cream. Most tortie cats are female.

Hair types

Cats of different breeds have varying hair lengths. Some have long, thick hair that requires regular grooming, while others have short hair that is easy to maintain. A few breeds have curly hair (called Rex) or very little hair at all (known as hairless).

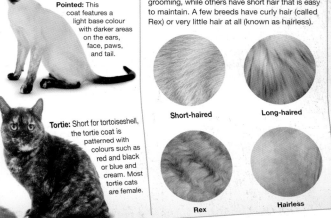

Short-haired

Long-haired

Rex

Hairless

A cat's tongue is covered in tiny, curved spines called

papillae

that help it to feed, drink, groom, and cool itself

SHARP TONGUE
The papillae on a cat's tongue help it to swallow running water. These backward-facing spines are made of a protein called keratin and feel like sandpaper, making them ideal for scraping meat from bones. They also work as a comb to clean fur.

Strong senses

Cats have heightened senses to suit their predatory lifestyle. They have excellent vision that is especially sensitive to movement and most effective at night. Their large, moveable ears can detect a range of sounds and pinpoint prey. Whiskers enhance the sense of touch, allowing cats to navigate through tight spaces.

Hearing

Cats are capable of hearing very high-pitched sounds, which can be inaudible to humans. The parts of the cat's brain that deal with sound are large and well developed.

A caracal's ears, among the largest of all felines, can detect a desert rodent's quiet footsteps and loud squeaking.

Caracal

Touch

Sensory hairs help cats move around, especially in the dark. Thick, stiff whiskers can judge the width of spaces, and hairs on the body and legs, called tylotrichs, help with climbing and measuring distances.

A cat uses its whiskers to move through a narrow space

Taste and smell

Cats are carnivores, so they have a limited taste for sweet foods. They analyse the individual scents of other cats by turning up their lips and inhaling deeply in what is known as the Flehmen response.

A lion's Flehmen response

Sight

All domestic cats have slit pupils (dark areas in the centre of each eye) as do many wild cats, but many of the larger cats have round pupils. Slit-eye vision allows the pupils to enlarge at night, letting light flood in, to help with hunting. It also helps with constriction to a very narrow slit in bright sunlight.

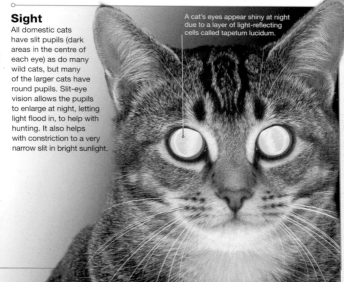

A cat's eyes appear shiny at night due to a layer of light-reflecting cells called tapetum lucidum.

Natural instincts

From the fight for survival in the wild to the safe haven of the back garden, cats share the same natural instincts. They are expert hunters that mark their territory and vocalize their feelings. Although domestic cats live with people, their behaviour is wild at heart and remains similar to that of the big cats.

Balancing act

Cats are acrobatic and agile creatures, capable of squeezing into tiny spaces and navigating narrow surfaces. Most cats can climb and sleep on trees, using their flexible spines and long tails for balance.

Cat fight

A fight-or-flight response provides self-defence in a scary situation. If fleeing a threat does not work, a cat fights back – especially in the case of females protecting young and males defending territories and mates.

Leopard sleeps on a branch

Marking territory

Cats scratch trees to sharpen their claws and to mark their territory. They also spray urine and deposit droppings. Wild cats have large territories that cannot be permanently patrolled, so they use scent markings to warn rivals.

Scared cat falling from a height

Head turns instinctively followed by front legs

Legs are extended to prepare for a hard landing

Righting reflex

A flexible spine allows a falling cat to quickly turn mid-air in order to land feet first – this is called a righting reflex. Although all cats have this ability, falling is scary for a cat and it can get hurt. For these reasons it is seldom seen and not something you should try out for yourself.

Kittens instinctively

curl up and stay still

when picked up by the scruff of their necks

Feline friends

Cats have enjoyed a special relationship with people since ancient times. Their independent spirit and affectionate nature make them perfect pets. They are adaptable, and form lasting bonds with their owners.

Sacred cats

Cats were sacred in ancient Egypt, and were believed to be the protectors of the pharaoh (ruler). Many cats are seen painted on tombs. The cat-headed goddess Bastet, protector of cats, was worshipped by the ancient Egyptians. When a treasured cat died, its body was mummified and laid to rest in an elaborate tomb.

Bronze statue of a cat, with gold on its eyes, from ancient Egypt

Pet cats on a vintage poster from 1894

Popular pets

About 9,000 years ago, cats hunted rodents and other pests on farms. This marked the start of their association with people. Today, cats are seen as beloved house pets all over the world.

Therapeutic pets

Cats love being stroked and cuddled. A purring cat is believed to have therapeutic benefits for its owner, including reduced stress and increased relaxation. Cats are often taken to hospitals and care homes for people to pet.

Stroking cats can lower blood pressure in humans.

Cat care

Cats should be registered with a local vet for regular health checks, vaccinations, booster shots, and so that a vet is available in case of an emergency. A microchip inserted under the cat's skin contains the owner's details to help identify a lost pet.

Vet examines a cat's eyes

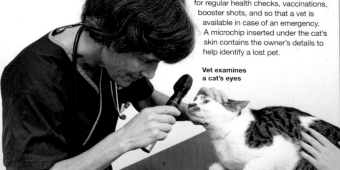

Cat groups

Most of the world's feline pets are the result of breeding without human interference. This produces the broad mix of domestic cats commonplace today. However, when specialist cat breeders get involved, a range of pedigrees, crossbreeds, and hybrids are created.

Pedigree cats

These cats have been bred specially to showcase particular physical traits or positive behaviours. Both their parents belong to the same breed. Each breed has its own unique appearance and personality.

A mixed-breed cat

The Asian Smoke breed is playful and intelligent

Non-pedigree cats

Any cat without a recorded ancestry is considered a non-pedigree, because its specific origins are unknown. Street cats and feral cats also belong to this group. In the UK, non-pedigrees are sometimes called "moggies".

This Bengal cat, a hybrid, is a cross between an Asian leopard cat and a domestic cat.

Lion, a large wild cat

Crossbreeds and hybrids

A cat with parents that belong to two different breeds is a crossbreed. However, crossing a domestic cat with a small wild cat of a different species produces a hybrid. Both crosses may be used to develop new breeds.

Wild cats

As their name suggests, wild cats in nature live free from humans and any form of domestication. They must hunt in order to survive, but loss of prey and reduced habitat is affecting their numbers – many of them are now endangered species.

Inherited traits

Cat breeders have long known that characteristics, such as coat colour, are passed from parent to offspring. They use selective breeding to create breeds with desirable features, but they must also consider inherited health problems.

Persian cats pass on their luxurious coats to their kittens

Domestic cats

Any cat that has been tamed to live alongside humans is considered domesticated. Cats have become much-loved pets in most parts of the world. They enjoy the creature comforts of a regular food supply, safe shelter, and human companionship.

CLOWDER
A group of cats is known as a clowder. Newborn cats or cats under a year old are called kittens, and male cats are called toms.

Domestic cats

Derived from the African wildcat (*Felis lybica*), the domestic cat is the only member of the Felidae family that lives with people. There are huge numbers of cats in the world, most of which are non-pedigree. Feral cats are not owned by anyone and live wild. Pedigree cats are a more recent development and make popular pets.

Cat on the hunt

Cat and mouse

Cats first came in contact with humans several thousand years ago when farmers began storing grain, attracting rats, which in turn attracted the African wildcat. Accepting this cat helped the farmers control rodents and other pests. Over time, cats were taken into the family home and became pets.

Global cats

Domestic cats spread all over the world when explorers and settlers introduced them to countries without existing cat populations. There are now more than 100 different breeds of domestic cat across the planet.

Cornish Rex, a curly-haired cat

Norwegian Forest Cat, a long-haired cat

Playtime

Domestic cats are among the world's most popular pets because they are loving, sociable, and playful. Cats need playtime to keep stimulated and to get exercise. Toys, scratching posts, and catnip are all cat favourites.

Cat playing with toy

Cleaning up

Cats clean their own fur regularly. However, long-haired domestic cats are bathed more frequently than short-haired ones, and are groomed almost every day to maintain hygiene and ensure their fur stays untangled. Hairless cats must have their sensitive skin bathed too.

Brushing a long-haired cat

A cat's whiskers
are sensitive to the
**slightest
change**
in air currents

FELINE WHISKERS
Whiskers are modified sensory hairs on a cat's face, with a rich supply of blood and nerve endings where they are rooted, deep inside the skin. Cats depend on their whiskers to detect objects that are too close for them to see clearly and to find a safe path in the dark.

Short-haired cats

Most domestic cats have naturally short hair, and unlike long-haired cats, they can keep their coats tangle-free and hunt successfully. Many short-haired breeds have been selectively bred from ordinary domestic cats over the last 100 years.

FOCUS ON...
WHISKERS

Whiskers are long sensory hairs on the face of a cat that are particularly useful to a night hunter.

▲ Most cats have long, straight, mobile whiskers that help them find their way in the dark.

▲ Curly whiskers are most often seen in Rex breeds. They are brittle and can break easily.

▲ Some cats, such as the hairless Sphynx, have short, fine whiskers or no whiskers at all.

American Shorthair

Domestic cats are said to have accompanied settlers to the USA in the 1600s, where they were kept as farm cats. By the 20th century, the cat was refined into a breed, which was formally recognized as the American Shorthair in the 1960s.

ORIGIN USA

WEIGHT 3.5–7 kg (8–15 lb)

COAT Most self colours and shades; patterns include bicolour, tabby, and tortie

American Wirehair

This breed originated in 1966 from a farm kitten born with a wiry coat. The American Wirehair has a dense coat in which every hair is crimped or bent at the end, giving it a distinctively rough texture.

ORIGIN USA

WEIGHT 3.5–7 kg (8–15 lb)

COAT Variety of self colours and shades in patterns including bicolour, tabby, and tortie

California Spangled

The California Spangled is known for its spotted coat, which resembles that of spotted wild cats. It was developed from domestic breeds in the 1970s in the hope that people would not want to wear fur that resembled their pet cat. The California Spangled was introduced to the public in 1986, but remains rare.

ORIGIN USA

WEIGHT 4–7 kg (9–15 lb)

COAT Dark spotted tabby with base colours including silver, bronze, gold, red, blue, black, brown, charcoal, and white

Munchkin

This small breed has much shorter legs than most domestic pedigree cats. Although the Munchkin's legs are about half the length of those of other cats, it can move surprisingly fast. This cat is found in short-haired and long-haired versions.

ORIGIN USA

WEIGHT 2.5–4 kg (6–9 lb)

COAT All colours, shades, and patterns

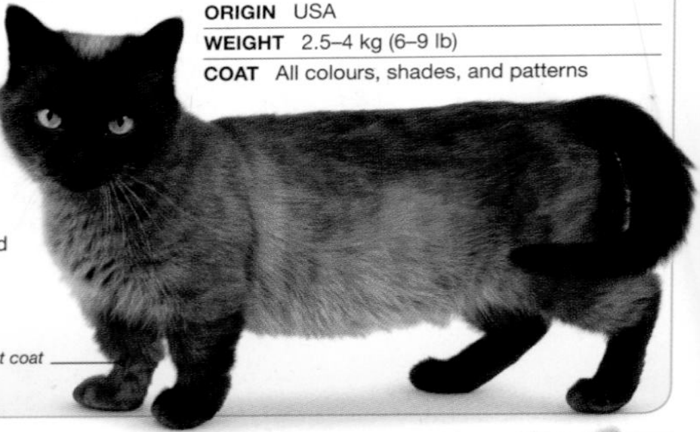

Mink colourpoint coat

Exotic Shorthair

The Exotic Shorthair was developed from Persian cats, and shares their flat face and sweet character. However, its fur is far shorter and does not need as much brushing.

ORIGIN USA

WEIGHT 3.5–7 kg (8–15 lb)

COAT Almost all colours and patterns

Bombay

The jet-black Bombay was bred by crossing black American Shorthairs with sable (dark brown) Burmese cats. The result is a muscular cat with a round head, copper eyes, glossy fur, and an affectionate nature.

ORIGIN USA

WEIGHT 2.5–5 kg (6–11 lb)

COAT Black only

The Bombay was the first breed specifically developed to look like a miniature Indian black leopard.

Snowshoe

The sweet Snowshoe gets its name from its pure white paws. This rare breed is related to the Siamese cat and shares its love of chatting and company.

ORIGIN USA

WEIGHT 2.5–5.5 kg (6–12 lb)

COAT Typical Siamese colours in pointed pattern

The Snowshoe breed started in the 1960s when a Siamese gave birth to three kittens with white paws.

Darker pointing similar to Siamese markings

Ocicat

Short, sleek, chocolate tabby coat

This cat comes from Siamese and Abyssinian ancestry. It is an athletic and talkative breed that combines the looks of a wild cat with the gentle nature of a domestic pet.

ORIGIN USA

WEIGHT 2.5–6.5 kg (6–14 lb)

COAT Black, brown, blue, lilac, and fawn, in spotted tabby patterns

Havana

A beautiful brown coat and affectionate nature earned this breed the nickname "chocolate delight". The Havana was first created in the UK in the 1950s by crossing Siamese and domestic short-haired cats. The American variant, which did not use the Siamese, has a rounder head.

ORIGIN UK/USA

WEIGHT 2.5–4.5 kg (6–10 lb)

COAT Rich brown and lilac

Vivid green eyes

Toyger

Although the Toyger was bred to resemble a toy tiger, it does not have the wild temperament of big cats. Its striped pattern comes from crossing a Bengal with a striped domestic shorthair. With tigerlike vertical stripes, its coat is unique among domestic breeds.

ORIGIN USA

WEIGHT 5.5–10 kg (12–22 lb)

COAT Brown mackerel tabby only

Short, lush coat

Lykoi

The unique appearance of this breed earned it the nickname "wolf cat". Patchy fur and large, pointed ears give this cat a wild, wolfish look. The Lykoi evolved from a natural mutation (random error in DNA) in feral cats.

ORIGIN USA

WEIGHT 2–4.5 kg (4.5–10 lb)

COAT Black mixed with white

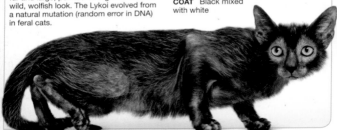

Tonkinese

This breed is the result of crossing Burmese and Siamese cats in the 1950s. The elegant, slender body and long legs are much more muscular than they look.

ORIGIN USA

WEIGHT 2.5–5.5 kg (6–12 lb)

COAT All colours except cinnamon and fawn, in pointed, tabby, and tortie patterns

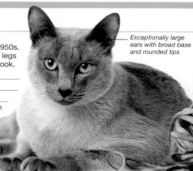

Exceptionally large ears with broad base and rounded tips

Serengeti

The Serengeti has the long neck and legs of a serval, a type of wild cat, and the same adventurous spirit. It is named after a part of Africa where wild cats live.

ORIGIN USA

WEIGHT 3.5–7 kg (8–15 lb)

COAT Black self colour, spotted tabby in shades of brown and silver, and black smoke

Scottish Fold

Neat, folded ears are a defining feature of the Scottish Fold. A kitten born in 1961 with folded ears, due to a mutation, was used to develop this unique breed.

ORIGIN UK/USA

WEIGHT 2.5–6 kg (6–13 lb)

COAT Most colours, shades, and patterns, including pointed, tabby, and tortie

Oriental – Bicolour

The high-energy Oriental cat is known to be very vocal, and benefits from both outdoor adventures and indoor play. The Bicolour comes in a wide range of colours and patterns, but always has white areas of fur on its body.

ORIGIN	USA
WEIGHT	4–6.5 kg (9–14 lb)
COAT	Various colours, shades, and patterns, including tabby, tortie, and some colourpoints; always with white areas

Oriental – Tortie

This cat's colourful tortoiseshell coat is the result of crossing solid-coloured Oriental Selfs with Tortie Siamese cats. The Oriental Tortie has green eyes and a firm, medium-sized body. Cats of this breed with a chocolate coat (shown here) are warm brown mixed with shades of red.

ORIGIN	UK
WEIGHT	4–6.5 kg (9–14 lb)
COAT	Black, blue, chocolate, lilac, fawn, cinnamon, and caramel, in tortie patterns

Oriental – Tabby

The Tabby variety of the Oriental breed is the result of crossing Siamese cats with non-pedigree tabbies. Like the rest of the Oriental breed, it is known to be highly intelligent and responsive to training.

ORIGIN USA

WEIGHT 4–6.5 kg (9–14 lb)

COAT All colours and shades in tabby and tortie-tabby patterns, mixed with white

Oriental – Foreign White

Breeders developed the Oriental breed in the UK during the 1950s from Asian cats. Although numerous coat colours and patterns occur in Oriental cats, the Foreign White stands out for its snow-white fur and blue eyes.

ORIGIN UK
WEIGHT 4–6.5 kg (9–14 lb)
COAT White only

Long, slim legs

Oriental – Cinnamon and Fawn

Slim, muscular body

The red-brown Cinnamon variety (shown here) is the result of a cross between a Siamese and an Abyssinian in the 1960s. The lighter brown Oriental Fawn coat was developed soon after. Wedge-shaped faces with large ears are common Oriental features.

ORIGIN UK
WEIGHT 4–6.5 kg (9–14 lb)
COAT Cinnamon and fawn

Long, thin, whiplike tail

Oriental – Smoke

Large ears with rounded tips

Glossy smoke coat

This cat's coat is made up of hairs that have two colour bands – the top band of the hair is a darker solid colour, such as black, and the bottom band is a paler colour. Both colours can be seen.

ORIGIN UK

WEIGHT 4–6.5 kg (9–14 lb)

COAT Self colours and tortie patterns

Oriental – Self

The Oriental Self's coat comes in a range of solid colours. This attention-seeking cat is intelligent, sociable, and lively. Like other Orientals, it is also much more vocal compared to other domestic breeds.

ORIGIN UK

WEIGHT 4–6.5 kg (9–14 lb)

COAT Cream, blue, lilac, ebony, red, and brown (also known as Havana)

Soft lilac coat

Asian – Self and Tortie

The Asian Self (shown here) is one solid colour, while the tortie variant has a tortoise-shell-like coat. This cat is known to be both vocal and affectionate.

ORIGIN UK

WEIGHT 4–7 kg (9–15 lb)

COAT All self colours and various tortie patterns

Asian – Tabby

In the 1980s, breeders crossed a Persian Chinchilla with a Burmese to develop the Asian Tabby. These cats have a tabby coat and are known for their shiny, patterned fur.

ORIGIN UK

WEIGHT 4–7 kg (9–15 lb)

COAT Various colours in tabby patterns

Asian – Smoke

The Smoke variety of this cat has a gleaming undercoat, which makes the fur appear to shimmer when it moves. This breed is naturally inquisitive.

ORIGIN UK

WEIGHT 4–7 kg (9–15 lb)

COAT Various colours and tortie patterns

Asian – Burmilla

This elegant cat was called "Burmilla" because of the accidental breeding of a lilac Burmese and a Persian Chinchilla, inspiring the breed's development. It is found in short-haired and long-haired versions.

ORIGIN	UK
WEIGHT	4–7 kg (9–15 lb)
COAT	Various colours

Black markings around the Burmilla's eyes look as though the cat is wearing eyeliner.

A kitten can sleep for up to

20 hours

a day for the first seven
days of its life

CAT NAP
Wild cats are most active at dawn and dusk, and do most of their hunting then and overnight. During the day, they sleep and rest – sometimes for 15 hours. Domestic cats have humans to provide their food and so are active during the day, but still sleep for long periods.

British Shorthair – Self

The most popular pedigree cat in the UK is the British Shorthair. A round face, powerfully built body, sturdy legs, short fur, and friendly nature are common in all varieties. The Self has a solid colour coat.

ORIGIN UK

WEIGHT 4–8 kg (9–18 lb)

COAT All self colours

Short, dense black coat with no white markings

British Shorthair – Bicolour

The Bicolour comes in a range of two-colour combinations and is prized for its almost symmetrical markings. British Shorthairs are affectionate, and this pleasant personality is what makes the breed a favourite for family pets.

ORIGIN UK

WEIGHT 4–8 kg (9–18 lb)

COAT All self colours with white, including blue, red, black, and cream

White and blue coat

British Shorthair – Tabby

Ancestors of the British Shorthairs roamed the farms and streets of England in the 19th century, and were kept to hunt rodents. The best working cats were selected and bred to produce the cat we see today. The striped Tabby features the same short, dense fur, which is easy for cat owners to maintain.

Classic red tabby coat

ORIGIN UK

WEIGHT 4–8 kg (9–18 lb)

COAT All traditional tabby patterns in many colours; tortie-tabby in various colours; both include silver variations

British Shorthair – Smoke

The eye-catching Smoke has a dark topcoat with a lighter undercoat. Beneath the fur lies a powerful, muscular body that needs regular exercise to stay strong and healthy.

ORIGIN UK

WEIGHT 4–8 kg (9–18 lb)

COAT All self colours, and tortie and pointed patterns

British Shorthair – Tortie and White

Areas of tortie patterns are clearly defined

The original Tortie variant of the British Shorthair was black mixed with red. Another longstanding coat colour is blue and cream. This cat now comes in a number of coats in which two colours are softly blended into one another. The Tortie and White variety (shown here) has patches of white on the coat.

ORIGIN	UK
WEIGHT	4–8 kg (9–18 lb)
COAT	Blue-cream, chocolate, lilac, or black tortoiseshell, with white patches on Tortie and White

British Shorthair – Tipped

The hairs in this cat's fur have coloured tips, giving it a light sprinkling of colour on top of a pale undercoat. It has big eyes and a round face. This variety also has a lush coat, and is sometimes likened to a cuddly teddy bear.

ORIGIN	UK
WEIGHT	4–8 kg (9–18 lb)
COAT	Various colours, including black-tipped on white or golden undercoat, and red-tipped on white undercoat

Short, sturdy neck and round face

British Shorthair – Colourpointed

The Colourpoint variety has bright blue eyes and a pale body, with darker colouring on the face, ears, tail, and paws. This colouring is the result of crossing British Shorthairs with the Siamese breed.

ORIGIN	UK
WEIGHT	4–8 kg (9–18 lb)
COAT	Various point colours, including blue-cream, seal, red, chocolate, and lilac; tabby and tortie patterns can also be found

Chartreux

The Chartreux is strong and agile, with a slightly woolly blue coat and a "smiling" expression. Although it is less active than most breeds, this cat is an excellent hunter.

ORIGIN	France
WEIGHT	3–7.5 kg (7–17 lb)
COAT	Blue-grey only

European Shorthair

Bred in Sweden during the early 1980s, the European Shorthair shares much in common with the British Shorthair. This active cat has a round face and muscular body.

Dense coat

ORIGIN	Sweden
WEIGHT	3.5–7 kg (8–15 lb)
COAT	Various self, smoke, and bicolours; in colourpoint, tabby, and tortie patterns

Thai

First bred to resemble a traditional Siamese of the 1950s, the Thai was later developed with a more extreme elongated appearance. This chatty cat follows its owner around and is always ready for play.

ORIGIN	Europe
WEIGHT	2.5–5.5 kg (6–12 lb)
COAT	Any point colours with pale ground colour

Almond-shaped blue eyes

Abyssinian

The exact origins of the Abyssinian remain unknown, but this old breed is often compared to African wildcats. This cat has a graceful, athletic body suited to its adventurous spirit and enthusiasm for exploring.

ORIGIN Ethiopia

WEIGHT 4–7.5 kg (9–17 lb)

COAT Several colours with distinct ticking (alternating bands of colour along a hair shaft) and facial markings

This cat is named after Abyssinia, an ancient kingdom that included Ethiopia and Eritrea.

Egyptian Mau

While this cat bears a
strong resemblance to the
cats seen in ancient Egyptian
tomb paintings, it is not directly
related to them. Its name, "Mau",
means "cat" in Egyptian. This
spotted cat is an affectionate
and playful pet.

ORIGIN Egypt

SIZE 2.5–5 kg (6–11 lb)

COAT Black, silver, bronze,
and black smoke, in spotted
tabby pattern

Arabian Mau

Originally a desert dweller in the hot
Arabian peninsula, the Arabian Mau
became domesticated after the breed
moved into towns while scavenging
for food. Selective breeding of this cat
began in 2004 with the aim of preserving
its original traits and natural hardiness,
which had developed as a result of living
alongside humans on the city streets.

ORIGIN United Arab Emirates

SIZE 3–7 kg (7–15 lb)

COAT Various self colours
and patterns, including
tabby and bicolour

The Arabian Mau was not recognized as a breed until 2008.

Australian Mist

Wide-based ears that tilt forward slightly

The "mist" in this short-haired cat's name comes from the ticking on its delicate, shiny coat. It was originally called the "Spotted Mist", but its name eventually changed to the "Australian Mist" when its marbled tabby coat pattern was accepted into the breed.

ORIGIN Australia

WEIGHT 3.5–6 kg (8–13 lb)

COAT Spotted or marbled tabby, misted by ticking; colours include brown, blue, peach, chocolate, lilac, and gold

Soft, sleek, glossy coat

The Australian Mist was the first pedigree breed to be developed entirely in Australia.

Neat, oval paws give this cat a sense of sure-footedness.

Russian Blue

Many believe that this beautiful breed
originated in the 1800s in a Russian city
called Archangel, close to the Arctic Circle.
It is known for its plush double coat and
green eyes, and is graceful and affectionate.
The Russian Blue is considered to be lucky
in Russia.

ORIGIN Russia

WEIGHT 3.5–5 kg (8–11 lb)

COAT Blue of various shades

Manx

Strong and sturdy body is compact in size

The Manx was developed on the Isle of Man, off the British coast, from kittens that were born without tails. This natural mutation (random change in DNA) in the cat population was known for at least 200 years before the Manx was formally recognized as a breed. This short-haired cat also has a long-haired version, called the Cymric.

ORIGIN UK

WEIGHT 3.5–5.5 kg (8–12 lb)

COAT All colours, shades, and patterns, including tabby and tortie

Short, dense tortie and white coat

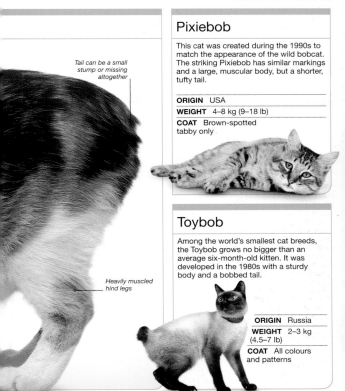

Tail can be a small stump or missing altogether

Heavily muscled hind legs

Pixiebob

This cat was created during the 1990s to match the appearance of the wild bobcat. The striking Pixiebob has similar markings and a large, muscular body, but a shorter, tufty tail.

ORIGIN USA

WEIGHT 4–8 kg (9–18 lb)

COAT Brown-spotted tabby only

Toybob

Among the world's smallest cat breeds, the Toybob grows no bigger than an average six-month-old kitten. It was developed in the 1980s with a sturdy body and a bobbed tail.

ORIGIN Russia

WEIGHT 2–3 kg (4.5–7 lb)

COAT All colours and patterns

Mekong Bobtail

Like all the bobtail breeds, the Mekong has an unusually short tail for a domestic cat. It has a colourpointed coat, much like the Siamese breeds. This cat is named after the Mekong River that runs through its homeland of Southeast Asia.

Short coat with very little undercoat

ORIGIN	Southeast Asia
WEIGHT	3.5–6 kg (8–13 lb)
COAT	Colourpoints as Siamese

Kurilian Bobtail

The Kurilian Bobtail hails from the Kuril Islands in the Pacific Ocean where it has lived for centuries. Almost unknown in the rest of the world, this breed was recognized in 2012 and it is popular in mainland Russia. Its thick topcoat and protective undercoat provide much needed warmth in cold climates. It also comes in a long-haired version.

Dense fur covering a compact, muscular body

ORIGIN	Kuril Islands, Russia
WEIGHT	3–4.5 kg (7–10 lb)
COAT	Most self colours and shades, in bicolour, tortie, and tabby patterns

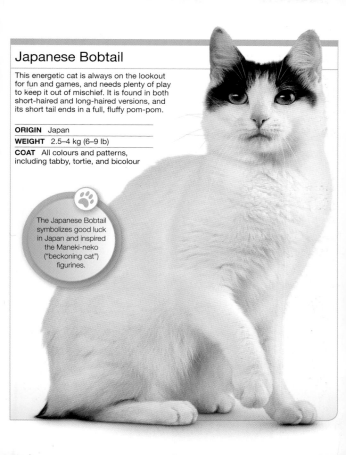

Japanese Bobtail

This energetic cat is always on the lookout for fun and games, and needs plenty of play to keep it out of mischief. It is found in both short-haired and long-haired versions, and its short tail ends in a full, fluffy pom-pom.

ORIGIN Japan

WEIGHT 2.5–4 kg (6–9 lb)

COAT All colours and patterns, including tabby, tortie, and bicolour

The Japanese Bobtail symbolizes good luck in Japan and inspired the Maneki-neko ("beckoning cat") figurines.

Korat

The Korat is among the oldest domestic cat breeds. In its native Thailand, this beautiful silver-blue cat is seen as a symbol of luck and a bringer of happiness.

ORIGIN Thailand

WEIGHT 2.5–5.5 kg (6–12 lb)

COAT Blue only

This breed is named after the Korat region of northeast Thailand, where it was first discovered.

Close-lying blue coat

Siamese – Tortie-Pointed

The sophisticated Siamese cat now has many different colour variations, including these points of mottled pattern. Most Tortie-Pointed Siamese are highly vocal and curious female felines that make their presence felt.

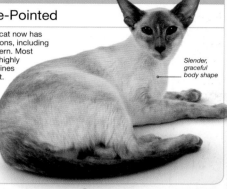

Slender, graceful body shape

ORIGIN UK

WEIGHT 2.5–5.5 kg (6–12 lb)

COAT Many tortie point colours, including seal, blue, chocolate, lilac, caramel, cinnamon, and fawn

Siamese – Tabby-Pointed

This Siamese coat with tabby point markings on a pale base colour was first seen in the early 20th century and soon grew popular. The Tabby-Pointed variety is also known as the Lynx Colourpoint in the USA.

This Siamese cat has a red tabby point coat.

ORIGIN UK

WEIGHT 2.5–5.5 kg (6–12 lb)

COAT Many tabby point colours, including chocolate, blue, and red; also in various tabby-tortie point colours

As Siamese kittens grow, their

face, ears, legs, and tail darken

Siamese – Self-Pointed

The Self-Pointed variety of the lively Siamese has a cream body contrasting a darker face, legs, and tail. The name comes from the royal courts of Siam, now Thailand, where the breed was developed many centuries ago.

ORIGIN Thailand

WEIGHT 2.5–5.5 kg (6–12 lb)

COAT All self colours in pointed patterns

Long, thin tail tapers to a point

Ceylon

This rare breed has striking yellow to green eyes and attractive tabby markings on its coat. A friendly cat, the Ceylon has a playful personality. It is named after its native country Ceylon, now called Sri Lanka.

ORIGIN Sri Lanka

WEIGHT 4–7.5 kg (9–17 lb)

COAT Shades of sand to gold with ticking of various colours

Short, silky fur is easy to keep clean.

Khao Manee

The "White Jewel", as its name translates, is a breed native to Thailand. It is known for its jewel-like bright eyes that can sometimes be odd-coloured. In past centuries, this rare cat was highly prized by the royal family in Thailand.

Odd-coloured eyes can be blue, green, or gold

ORIGIN	Thailand
WEIGHT	2.5–5.5 kg (6–12 lb)
COAT	White only

White cats are described in *Tamra Maew*, a book of cat poems from 14th-century Thailand.

Shiny, pure white coat

American Burmese

Burmese cats are sometimes called "bricks wrapped in silk" because they have surprisingly heavy bodies and silky smooth fur. The American Burmese was bred in the USA from a similar cat brought in from Myanmar (Burma).

ORIGIN Myanmar/USA

WEIGHT 3.5–6.5 kg (8–14 lb)

COAT Self and tortie colours in sepia pattern (gradual shading to dark colour)

Full, round head

Short, silky, chocolate coat

European Burmese

In the 1940s, European breeders developed the European Burmese from some American Burmese cats imported from the USA. The main difference between the Burmese breeds is the European's wedge-shaped head, which is longer than the American's rounder head. This cat loves companionship and needs a lot of affection.

ORIGIN USA/Europe

WEIGHT 3.5–6.5 kg (8–14 lb)

COAT Self and tortie colours including blue, brown, cream, lilac, and red in sepia pattern

Ancestors of the Burmese cats lived as temple cats in Myanmar 600 years ago.

Smooth, reddish coat

Rex cats

Cats with curly coats are the result of a mutation (random change in DNA), which is passed on through selective breeding. Although their coats can look similar, each Rex breed has its own unique mutation.

FOCUS ON...
HAIRS
Cats have up to three types of hair in their coats. Each one provides different protection.

Cornish Rex

In 1950, the Cornish Rex was developed from a curly haired kitten born in Cornwall, UK. This breed's ancestors once hunted rodents on farms. Today it is content to snuggle in its owner's lap and play games.

ORIGIN	UK
WEIGHT	2.5–4 kg (6–9 lb)
COAT	All self and shaded colours and patterns, including tabby, tortie, colourpoint, and bicolour

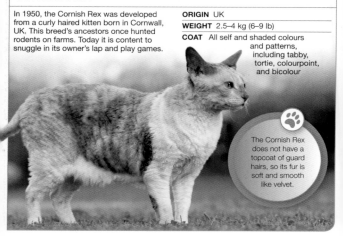

The Cornish Rex does not have a topcoat of guard hairs, so its fur is soft and smooth like velvet.

▲ Down hairs are short and soft, covering the body in a snuggly undercoat to keep the cat warm.

▲ Awn hairs are stiff and bristly, with thickened tips to ensure the cat is not easily injured.

▲ Guard hairs are thick and coarse, creating a waterproof top layer to keep the cat dry.

Devon Rex

A decade after the Cornish Rex was discovered, another curly haired kitten was found in the neighbouring county of Devon, UK. This breed is also known as the "poodle cat" because its curly coat resembles that of a poodle dog.

ORIGIN UK

WEIGHT 2.5–4 kg (6–9 lb)

COAT All colours, shades, and patterns

German Rex

Among the rarer Rex breeds is the German variety. With much thicker awn hairs and no guard hairs, this cat's coat is woolly like that of a sheep.

Rounded head with broad-based ears

ORIGIN Germany

WEIGHT 2.5–4.5 kg (6–10 lb)

COAT All colours, shades, and patterns

Skookum

This experimental new breed combines the short legs of the Munchkin and the curly coat of the LaPerm. The name Skookum comes from an American Indian word meaning "powerful".

ORIGIN USA

WEIGHT 2.5–4 kg (6–9 lb)

COAT All colours and patterns

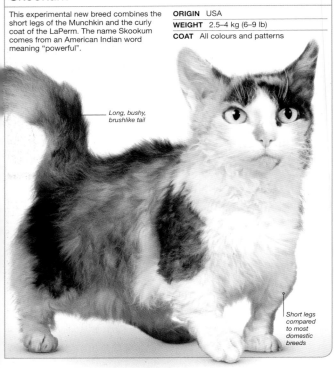

Long, bushy, brushlike tail

Short legs compared to most domestic breeds

LaPerm

A mutation (random change in DNA) in a farm cat produced the extremely fluffy LaPerm breed, which is known for its expert hunting skills. The cat's muscular body is covered in soft, springy curls, and it even has a set of wavy whiskers.

ORIGIN USA

WEIGHT 3.5–5.5 kg (8–12 lb)

COAT All colours, shades, and patterns

The longest, tightest curls are in the thick ruff surrounding the neck.

Selkirk Rex

The first Selkirk Rex was a curly coated kitten found at a Montana animal rescue centre in the USA. Kittens of this breed have fur that straightens out briefly, before curling again as it grows older. The curls can take up to two years to develop fully.

ORIGIN USA

WEIGHT 3–5 kg (7–11 lb)

COAT All colours, shades, and patterns

Thick, shaggy coat of a five-month-old kitten

FURRY FELINES
The cuddly Maine Coon has long, thick fur with a dense neck ruff and bib, and a long, bushy tail. The long, silky guard hairs keep the coat waterproof, while the dense undercoat of awn and down hairs keep the cat warm in icy conditions.

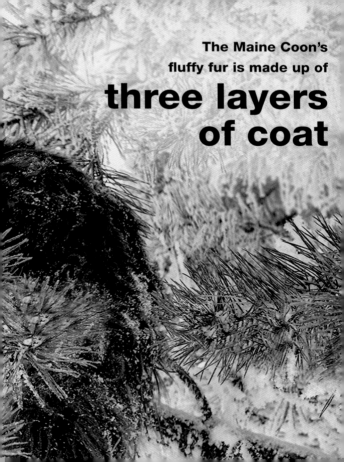

The Maine Coon's
fluffy fur is made up of

three layers of coat

Long-haired cats

The first known long-haired cats lived many centuries ago in Central Asia. Long hair in cats may have developed as a natural mutation (random change in DNA) in response to cold climates. The thick, fluffy fur of these breeds requires regular grooming to keep it untangled and soft.

Maine Coon

The heavyweight Maine Coon hails from the American state of Maine, and is one of the oldest and largest cat breeds in the country. It relies on its thick, waterproof coat, which is especially thick around its neck, to keep warm.

ORIGIN   USA

WEIGHT   4–7.5 kg (9–17 lb)

COAT   Self colours and shades, in tortie, tabby, and bicolour patterns

In 2004, a Maine Coon called "Little Nicky" became the first cat to be cloned commercially.

Ragdoll

Despite its large size, this blue-eyed breed is said to go limp and floppy like a rag doll when it is picked up, hence its name. The cat has a relaxed nature, and loves having its silky soft fur stroked and brushed.

Woolly undercoat is overlaid with long, silky guard hairs

Long, plumed tail

ORIGIN USA

SIZE 4.5–9 kg (10–20 lb)

COAT Most self colours in tortie and tabby patterns, but always pointed and bicolour or mitted (white paws)

Somali

The first Somali cats were long-haired versions of the Abyssinian breed. Highly active with an athletic body and adventurous spirit, this cat likes to climb and explore. It has a friendly and affectionate nature, and makes an amusing pet.

ORIGIN USA

WEIGHT 3.5–5.5 kg (8–12 lb)

COAT Various colours, some with silver tipping; tortie pattern; silver hairs always ticked

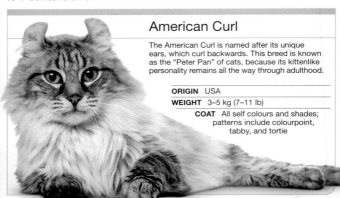

American Curl

The American Curl is named after its unique ears, which curl backwards. This breed is known as the "Peter Pan" of cats, because its kittenlike personality remains all the way through adulthood.

ORIGIN USA

WEIGHT 3–5 kg (7–11 lb)

COAT All self colours and shades; patterns include colourpoint, tabby, and tortie

York Chocolate

This breed is still relatively rare. It is named after its origins in the US state of New York and its chocolate brown fur. Most York Chocolate cats are affectionate lap cats that love to be petted.

Lustrous long fur is silky soft to the touch

ORIGIN USA

WEIGHT 2.5–5 kg (6–11 lb)

COAT Self colour: lavender, chocolate; bicolour: white and chocolate, and lavender and white

American Bobtail

In the 1960s, a litter of bobtail kittens were born to a Siamese cat and a short-tailed tabby. One of the kittens had a short tail, and eventually it was crossed with other cats to produce the American Bobtail breed.

ORIGIN USA

WEIGHT 3–7 kg (7–15 lb)

COAT All colours, shades, and patterns, including tabby, tortie, and colourpoint

Short, slightly curved tail

Highlander

With its thick, heavy, long-haired coat, this breed has the dramatic looks of a wild cat, but with curled ears. The Highlander also comes in a short-haired variety. It makes an affectionate pet.

ORIGIN USA

WEIGHT 4.5–11 kg (10–24 lb)

COAT All colours in any tabby pattern, including colourpoints

Highlander kittens are born with straight ears that curl back during the first few weeks of their lives.

Kinkalow

This cat is a result of crossing the American Curl with the Munchkin in the 1990s. It also comes in a short-haired version.

ORIGIN USA

WEIGHT 2.5–4 kg (6–9 lb)

COAT Many colours and patterns, including tabby and tortie

Persian – Colourpoint

Also known as the Himalayan, the Persian Colourpoint originated in 1931 from a cross between a Persian and a Siamese. This robust cat may look like a Persian, but it has a louder voice and is more outgoing.

ORIGIN USA

WEIGHT 3.5–7 kg (8–15 lb)

COAT Points in a variety of self colours, and also in tortie, tabby, and tortie-tabby patterns

Ragamuffin

The furry Ragamuffin is closely related to the Ragdoll. It shares the same calm nature as the Ragdoll, but its soft coat comes in a wider variety of colours and patterns.

Thick, plush coat needs regular grooming to avoid tangles

ORIGIN USA

WEIGHT 4.5–9 kg (10–20 lb)

COAT All self colours in bicolour, tortie, and tabby patterns

Balinese-Javanese

Long-haired Balinese-Javanese cats were developed by mixing the Balinese (a long-haired version of the Siamese) and the colourpoint shorthair breeds. They are recognized by their luxurious fur and large, plumelike tail.

ORIGIN USA

WEIGHT 2.5–5 kg (6–11 lb)

COAT Many point colours in tabby and tortie patterns

Long, soft coat is silky to the touch

Nebelung

The name of this rare breed is German for "creature of the mist", a reference to the Nebelung's thick, silky fur, which appears to float over its body. This quiet and gentle cat likes to stay at home with a regular routine.

Silver-tipped furry tail is longer than the entire body

ORIGIN USA

WEIGHT 2.5–5 kg (6–11 lb)

COAT Blue, sometimes silver-tipped

Balinese

The Balinese breed was developed from the Siamese in the 1950s and has similar pointed markings, but longer and thicker fur. This cat is known for its almond-shaped, deep-blue eyes. It has a slender body, dainty paws, and graceful movement.

ORIGIN USA

WEIGHT 2.5–5 kg (6–11 lb)

COAT Seal, chocolate, blue, and lilac self colourpoints

The elegant Balinese is named after traditional dancers on the island of Bali, Indonesia.

British Longhair

Also known as the Lowlander in the USA, this cat differs from the British Shorthair only in the length and thickness of its coat. The body size, shape, and colours remain the same.

Short, thick tail resembles a bristly brush

ORIGIN UK

WEIGHT 4–8 kg (9–18 lb)

COAT All traditional and pointed colours; bicolour, tabby, and tortie patterns

Chantilly/Tiffany

The rare Chantilly/Tiffany, so-called because of an early confusion in its naming, has a very full, silky, long coat and a long, plumed tail. This sweet-natured cat communicates with gentle chirping sounds.

ORIGIN USA

WEIGHT 2.5–5 kg (6–11 lb)

COAT Black, blue, lilac, chocolate, cinnamon, and fawn; various tabby patterns

Persian – Cameo Bicolour

The Persian, known for its flat face and flowing fur, may have originated in Persia, now called Iran. This variety of Persian has a light-coloured coat with white patches. The colour varies in shade depending on how far along the hair shaft from the tip it extends. The bases of the hairs are white.

ORIGIN USA, Australia, and New Zealand

WEIGHT 3.5–7 kg (8–15 lb)

COAT Most self colours and tortie patterns, but with white markings.

Persian – Cameo

The Persian Cameo is known for its rippling coat with softly blended colours. It likes to stay indoors and relax quietly in a calm household.

ORIGIN USA, Australia, and New Zealand

WEIGHT 3.5–7 kg (8–15 lb)

COAT Most self colours and tortie patterns

Persian – Self

This type of Persian has one solid fur colour. Some of the earliest Persians were white. Independent by nature, this cat enjoys its own company.

ORIGIN UK

WEIGHT 3.5–7 kg (8–15 lb)

COAT White, black, blue, red, cream, chocolate, and lilac

Persian – Chinchilla

The black tips on the Persian Chinchilla's silver-white coat give its fur a shimmery appearance. The cat's thick fur and woolly undercoat require regular brushing to remove tangles.

ORIGIN UK

WEIGHT 3.5–7 kg (8–15 lb)

COAT White with black tips

The Persian Chinchilla shot to fame when it appeared in several *James Bond* films.

Short nose

The Persian Blue
was a favourite
cat breed of
Queen
Victoria

ROYAL PETS

Persians have proved popular in royal history. Queen Victoria of the UK and King Louis XV of France both kept pet Persians. The Persian started out only in self colours, but has since been bred into a variety of colours and patterns.

Persian – Smoke

This type of Persian was developed in the late 1800s. Its stunning smoke fur is pale at the base and grows darker at the ends of each hair. Black smoke was one of the earliest colours of this breed, followed by blue and silver.

ORIGIN UK

WEIGHT 3.5–7 kg (8–15 lb)

COAT White deeply tipped with colour, including black, blue, cream, or red, and in tortie patterns

Persian – Smoke Bicolour

The Smoke Bicolour is just like the Smoke variety, but has white patches too. The cats with tortie patterns have two smoke colours with white. This cat's thick fur must be groomed daily to avoid it becoming dirty or tangled.

ORIGIN UK

WEIGHT 3.5–7 kg (8–15 lb)

COAT White with smoke colours, including tortie patterns

Persian – Bicolour

Over time, breeders have continued to develop the Persian coat to even greater lengths. One of the first Bicolours to be developed was black and white, once referred to as the "magpie".

ORIGIN UK

WEIGHT 3.5–7 kg (8–15 lb)

COAT White with various self colours, including black, red, blue, cream, chocolate, and lilac, and with tortie patterns

Well-defined colour patches across the body

Persian – Pewter

The Pewter variety of the Persian features light fur with contrasting darker tips. The eyes of this striking-looking cat range from deep orange to copper coloured.

ORIGIN	UK
WEIGHT	3.5–7 kg (8–15 lb)
COAT	Very pale colours with black or blue tipping

Persian – Silver Tabby

This early variety of the Persian originated during the 1800s. Bicolour Silver Tabbies have visible white areas on their muzzle, chest, and underparts.

ORIGIN	UK
WEIGHT	3.5–7 kg (8–15 lb)
COAT	Silver tabby, tortie silver tabby; both with white patches

Thick, fluffy fur needs daily brushing

Persian – Shaded Silver

The shimmering fur of this breed was developed in the 1800s. The coat is very similar to the Persian Chinchilla's, but has darker and more contrasting markings. One of the Shaded Silver's most striking features is its luminous blue-green eyes.

ORIGIN UK

WEIGHT 3.5–7 kg (8–15 lb)

COAT White with black tips

The Pokémon species named "Persian" is based on the Persian breed.

Persian – Tortie and Tortie & White

The Tortie variety of the Persian breed is very rare. The tortoiseshell pattern features different bands of colour in the long-haired coat, while distinctive patches of white are seen in the Tortie & White type.

ORIGIN UK

WEIGHT 3.5–7 kg (8–15 lb)

COAT Tortie colours, including lilac-cream and chocolate, also with white patches

Shades of red and black fur blend together in this tortie coat.

Persians have been nicknamed "furniture with fur" for their lazy, inactive lifestyle.

Persian – Golden

The first golden-haired kittens were initially disregarded because they were born to Chinchilla Persian cats, and so they were the wrong colour. Since then, the breed's rich, golden fur has gained widespread appeal, and it is now a much-prized pet.

ORIGIN UK

WEIGHT 3.5–7 kg (8–15 lb)

COAT Apricot to golden, with black or brown tips

Persian – Tabby and Tortie Tabby

Tabbies are the extroverts of the Persian breed, showing lots of personality. They appreciate games and interaction, and are more active than other Persian varieties. The tabby markings of the Tortie Tabbies lie on a bicoloured coat.

ORIGIN UK

WEIGHT 3.5–7 kg (8–15 lb)

COAT Many colours also with silver tipping in tabby and tortie-tabby patterns

Norwegian Forest Cat

After WWII, the Norse Skogkatt was declared the official cat of Norway and renamed as the Norwegian Forest Cat.

This fluffy feline has a thick fur coat that helps it to withstand the snowy conditions and freezing temperatures of Scandinavia. A thick, top layer keeps out the damp, while its woolly undercoat provides warmth.

ORIGIN Norway

WEIGHT 3–9 kg (7–20 lb)

COAT Most self colours, shades, and patterns

Aphrodite Giant

The mountains of Cyprus were the original home of the Aphrodite Giant. Males are considerably larger than females, and can have either semi-long or short coats. This long-legged breed is a capable climber, with a thick coat that can be long- or short-haired.

ORIGIN Cyprus

WEIGHT 4.5–8 kg (10–18 lb)

COAT Most solid colours; bicolour with irregular white markings

Oriental Longhair

This breed was originally called the English Angora. It was developed in the 1960s as a long-haired version of the Oriental Shorthair, and gained its current name in 2002. Its sleek coat lies flat against the body as it lacks a woolly undercoat.

ORIGIN UK

WEIGHT 2.5–5 kg (6–11 lb)

COAT Many self, smoke, and shaded colours; tortie, tabby, and bicolour patterns

Turkish Van

The ancestors of this cat were named after Lake Van in Turkey. This playful feline has a liking for water games, and some cats of this breed can be good swimmers.

ORIGIN UK/Turkey

WEIGHT 3–8.5 kg (7–19 lb)

COAT White with darker colours on head and tail

Darker fur on fluffy tail

Turkish Vankedisi

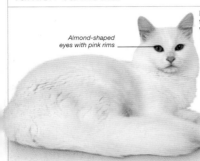

Almond-shaped eyes with pink rims

Prized for its snow-white coat, the Vankedisi differs from the Turkish Van only in the lack of darker colours on its head and tail. Like all white cats, this feline can also have odd-coloured eyes. Considered to be a rare breed all over the world, it is especially valued in its native country, Turkey.

ORIGIN	Eastern Turkey
WEIGHT	3–8.5 kg (7–19 lb)
COAT	Pure white only

Siberian Forest

This sturdy cat was bred to survive the harsh Russian climate. Although still rare, the Siberian Forest cat is gaining popularity for its good looks and engaging personality. The cat may take five years or more to grow fully into an adult.

Thick ruff around neck

ORIGIN	Russia
WEIGHT	4.5–9 kg (10–20 lb)
COAT	All colours and patterns

Turkish Angora

Recognized by its silky, shimmering coat, the Turkish Angora is considererd to be one of the most beautiful of all long-haired cats. This agile climber loves playing games and splashing in water. This cat has been widely used to develop Persian cats and other long-haired breeds.

ORIGIN	Turkey
WEIGHT	2.5–5 kg (6–11 lb)
COAT	Traditionally white; now many self colours and patterns

This much-loved cat features often on postage stamps and advertisements in Turkey.

Large, tufted ears sit high on head

Fine, silky coat with no undercoat

Black tortie smoke coat

DIFFERENT COLOURS
Heterochromia is an eye condition in which each iris is a different colour. In cats, it occurs almost entirely in felines that have the gene for white or white spotting colour. The gene reduces the amount of colour or pigment reaching the iris of one eye of a kitten during its development, causing heterochromia.

Cats with heterochromia always have

one blue eye,

while the other can be
green, yellow, or brown

Hairless cats

Hairlessness in cats is a natural mutation (random change in DNA). A hairless kitten born in 1966 was used to develop a breed of hairless cat called the Sphynx. Although these cats appear hairless, most are covered in a fine layer of fur. Hairless cats are mostly kept indoors to protect their skin from the sun or cold.

Sphynx

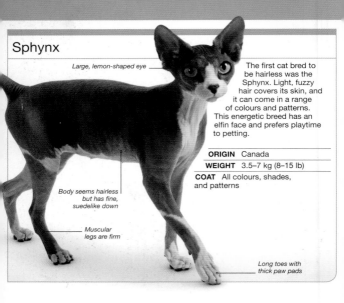

Large, lemon-shaped eye

The first cat bred to be hairless was the Sphynx. Light, fuzzy hair covers its skin, and it can come in a range of colours and patterns. This energetic breed has an elfin face and prefers playtime to petting.

ORIGIN Canada

WEIGHT 3.5–7 kg (8–15 lb)

COAT All colours, shades, and patterns

Body seems hairless but has fine, suedelike down

Muscular legs are firm

Long toes with thick paw pads

Bambino

Crossing the hairless Sphynx with the short-legged Munchkin resulted in the Bambino. This Italian name translates as "baby", which suits the short and sweet-tempered breed.

Very large, broad-based ears

ORIGIN	USA
WEIGHT	2–4 kg (4.5–9 lb)
COAT	All colours, shades, and patterns

Legs shorter than in most domestic breeds

Elf Cat

This new, rare breed was developed in the 21st century by crossing the Sphynx and the American Curl. The Elf Cat has barely any hair and ears that curl back. The wrinkled skin feels like chamois (soft leather) and has very fine, downy hair.

Loose skin creates wrinkles on the body

ORIGIN	USA
WEIGHT	3.5–7 kg (8–15 lb)
COAT	All colours, shades, and patterns

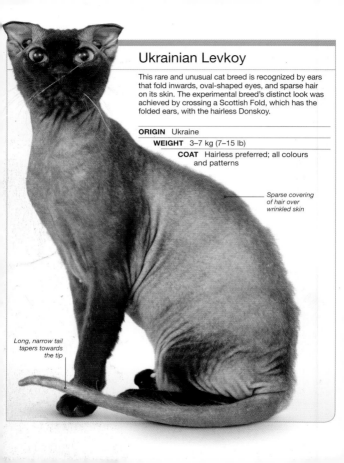

Ukrainian Levkoy

This rare and unusual cat breed is recognized by ears that fold inwards, oval-shaped eyes, and sparse hair on its skin. The experimental breed's distinct look was achieved by crossing a Scottish Fold, which has the folded ears, with the hairless Donskoy.

ORIGIN	Ukraine
WEIGHT	3–7 kg (7–15 lb)
COAT	Hairless preferred; all colours and patterns

Sparse covering
of hair over
wrinkled skin

Long, narrow tail
tapers towards
the tip

Peterbald

This unique cat was created in the 1990s by crossing the Oriental Shorthair with the Donskoy. It was so well-received in the Russian city of St Petersburg that it was named Peterbald. A layer of short, fine hair means this breed is not entirely hairless.

Huge ears compared to the head size

ORIGIN Russia

WEIGHT 3.5–7 kg (8–15 lb)

COAT All colours, shades, and patterns

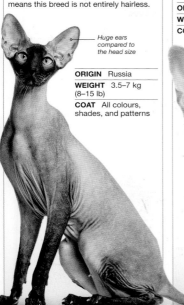

Donskoy

The Donskoy breed was developed from a nearly hairless cat discovered in the Russian city of Rostov-on-Don in 1987 – resulting in the breed's name.

ORIGIN Russia

WEIGHT 3.5–7 kg (8–15 lb)

COAT All colours, shades, and patterns

Large eyes compared to the small, wedge-shaped face

Hybrid cats

Crossing a domestic cat with a wild cat produces a hybrid. These exotic cats display the attractive markings of their wild relations. However, it can take generations of selective breeding to other cats before they can be sold as domestic pets.

FOCUS ON...
WILD PARENTS
Hybrid cats are the offspring of two different species – the domestic cat *Felis catus* and a wild cat species.

Chausie

The Chausie was developed from cats that were crossbred with a jungle cat. Later generations were crossed with selected domestic cats, especially the Abyssinian, to develop the cat we see today.

ORIGIN USA

WEIGHT 5.5–10 kg (12–22 lb)

COAT Black self and ticked tabby pattern in brown, and black with silver

Bengal

The popular Bengal captures the beauty and stunning patterns of the Asian leopard cat. This breed is naturally alert and endlessly energetic with a passion for exploring.

ORIGIN USA

WEIGHT 5.5–10 kg (12–22 lb)

COAT Brown, sepia, and snow colours, in spotted and marble classic tabby patterns

▲ The jungle cat was crossed with domestic cats to produce the Chausie breed.

▲ The Asian leopard cat was the wild parent of the hybrid that led to the creation of the Bengal breed.

▲ Native to Africa, the serval was used to produce the Savannah breed.

Savannah

The tallest domestic breed is the Savannah, which inherited the long legs, large ears, and spotted coat of the African serval. Adventurous by nature, this cat is a skilled climber and a fast runner.

ORIGIN USA

WEIGHT 5.5–10 kg (12–22 lb)

COAT Brown-spotted tabby, black silver-spotted tabby, black, or black smoke

The Bengal cat is the only domestic breed with a coat pattern of
rosettes

WILD ROSETTES
The Bengal cat was developed by crossing domestic breeds with the wild Asian leopard cat, from which it inherited its beautiful rosette pattern. Its markings look just like the camouflaged coats of cats in the wild.

Wild cats

From the world-famous big cats to the lesser-known small cats, wild cats live across a wide range of natural habitats. They must all hunt down prey, defend their territories, and survive the many challenges of life in the wild.

CAMOUFLAGED CATS
A variety of coat colours and patterns help wild cats blend into their surroundings. This lioness goes largely unnoticed in her grassland home.

Wild cats

There are 41 species of wild cat. Of these, the seven big cats, including the lion and tiger, are well known, but there are many more small wild cats. The largest wild cat is the Amur tiger, which weighs up to 300 kg (660 lb), while the smallest is the rusty-spotted cat. The males of this species weigh only 1.6 kg (3.5 lb).

Cat categories

Wild cats are divided into two groups: the Pantherinae, which are the big cats, and the Felinae, which includes the small wild cats and the domestic cat. Big cats live in Africa, Asia, and Central and South America, whereas smaller wild cats are found not only in these places but also in North America and Europe. While some big cats can roar, all small cats purr.

The cheetah is a small wild cat

Clever camouflage

Wild cats try to stay hidden while stalking unsuspecting prey. Their fur helps to camouflage them, letting them blend into their surroundings. They have striped, spotty, or sand-coloured fur, depending on their habitat – whether it is dense forests, open grasslands, sandy deserts, or snowy mountains.

A snow leopard in its habitat

Shared habits

Wild and domestic cats behave in similar ways – they are more active in the evening and learn survival skills through play when they are young. The main difference is that wild cats must hunt for food to survive, while domestic cats are fed and cared for by humans.

Tiger cubs at play

Small cats

Most wild cats around the world today are small cats. There are 34 species of small cat that live across a range of habitats. From their camouflaged coats to their agile athleticism, the bodies and lifestyles of these cats are perfectly adapted for survival in their habitats.

Serval
Leptailurus serval

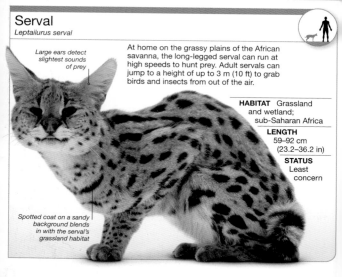

At home on the grassy plains of the African savanna, the long-legged serval can run at high speeds to hunt prey. Adult servals can jump to a height of up to 3 m (10 ft) to grab birds and insects from out of the air.

Large ears detect slightest sounds of prey

Spotted coat on a sandy background blends in with the serval's grassland habitat

HABITAT Grassland and wetland; sub-Saharan Africa

LENGTH 59–92 cm (23.2–36.2 in)

STATUS Least concern

Caracal
Caracal caracal

This cat has large black-furred ears with tufts up to 4.5 cm (1.7 in) long. Its tail is relatively short, only reaching its hocks (the joints in the back legs that point backwards). The caracal's name comes from the Turkish word "karakulak", which means "black ear".

HABITAT Dry wood and scrubland, savanna, and arid mountain areas; Africa and southern Asia

LENGTH 61–105 cm (24–41.3 in)

STATUS Least concern

Caracal's hock

The enormous ears of the serval cover almost all the top of its head. Their size reflects this cat's powerful sense of hearing. Servals can hear the high-pitched squeaks of rodents as well as the sounds they make as they run along the ground. They use this to detect the exact position of prey before pouncing.

Compared to all the other
wild cats, the serval has the

largest ears

relative to its size

Ocelot
Leopardus pardalis

This small, solitary cat feeds on rodents. Although ocelots mainly live and hunt on the ground, ocelots are also strong swimmers and can climb when necessary.

HABITAT Tropical and subtropical forest, and shrub woodland; North, Central, and South America

LENGTH 72–101 cm (28–40 in)

STATUS Least concern

Larger front paws help in climbing trees

Margay
Leopardus wiedii

Resembling a small ocelot, the margay lives in tropical forests where prey is plentiful. Most of its prey is tree-living and includes small mammals. This cat's long legs and tail help it to climb easily and stay balanced in the trees.

HABITAT Tropical forest; Central and South America

LENGTH 42–79 cm (17–31 in)

STATUS Near threatened

The margay can rotate its ankles 180 degrees allowing it to climb down trees head-first easily.

Geoffroy's Cat
Leopardus geoffroyi

This tiny cat sleeps in trees by day and hunts small mammals and birds at night. It was named after the 19th century French explorer Étienne Geoffroy Saint-Hilaire.

HABITAT Dry scrubland and woodland, grassland, and marsh; Central and South America

LENGTH
43–88 cm (17–34.6 in)

STATUS Least concern

Its patterned coat camouflages the cat in the dense trees and undergrowth.

Oncilla

Leopardus tigrinus

The oncilla is a rare species. This skilled hunter stalks its prey on the forest floor before pouncing to make the kill. It is a good climber and a nocturnal cat (mainly active at night).

HABITAT Forest and shrubland; Central and South America

LENGTH 38–57 cm (15–22.4 in)

STATUS Vulnerable

Asian Golden Cat

Catopuma temminckii

This powerful cat is a solid colour – brown, black-grey, and shades in between – over much of its range, but felines of this breed found in parts of China may have spots and stripes.

HABITAT Tropical and subtropical forest, grassland, and open rocky areas; China and Southeast Asia

LENGTH 66–105 cm (26–41.3 in)

STATUS Near threatened

Marbled Cat

Pardofelis marmorata

The marbled cat resembles a smaller version of the clouded leopard, with similar markings. This cat uses its long, bushy tail and broad feet for climbing and balancing on trees as it hunts birds, squirrels, rats, and frogs.

HABITAT Forest; southwest China, Malaysia, and Indonesia

LENGTH 45–62 cm (17.7–24 in)

STATUS Near threatened

The marbled cat is rarely seen because it lives in remote areas and is likely active at night.

Irregular pattern of black stripes and spots on the head

Canadian Lynx
Lynx canadensis

The Canadian Lynx has distinctively long ear tufts. It has large, furry feet that act like snowshoes in the winter and provide grip on the icy ground of its home.

HABITAT Forest and shrubland; Canada and USA

LENGTH 76–106 cm (30–41.7 in)

STATUS Least concern

Bobcat
Lynx rufus

This wild cat is a lynx, but with shorter ear tufts. It lives at high altitudes in rocky mountains, and has a spotted coat that provides camouflage.

HABITAT Forest, scrubland, and desert; Canada, USA, and Mexico

LENGTH 65–105 cm (26–41.3 in)

STATUS Least concern

Iberian Lynx
Lynx pardinus

The Iberian lynx is at home in the Iberian Peninsula of southwest Europe. It has a fluffy facial ruff, long ear tufts, and a black-tipped tail.

Prominent black ear tufts

HABITAT Open forest and shrubland; Spain

LENGTH 68–82 cm (27–32 in)

STATUS Endangered

Eurasian Lynx
Lynx lynx

This cat is the largest of the lynxes, and feeds mainly on smaller, hooved mammals rather than rabbits and hares as the other lynxes do. It is the third biggest predator in Europe, after the brown bear and wolf.

HABITAT Forest; Europe and Asia

LENGTH 80–110 cm (31.4–43.3 in)

STATUS Least concern

Puma

Puma concolor

The largest of the small wild cats is the powerful puma. This expert climber covers vast distances to hunt prey. It can make various sounds, but it cannot roar. The puma is known by many names, including cougar, red tiger, and mountain lion.

HABITAT Forest, mountain, desert, and grassland; North, Central, and South America

LENGTH 86–155 cm (34–61 in)

STATUS Least concern

Agile and extremely muscular body

For the Incas, a South American civilization, the puma was a symbol of courage and strength.

Jaguarundi
Herpailurus yagouaroundi

Red-brown coat colour provides effective camouflage in dense forest undergrowth

This small wild cat is also called "otter cat" because its slender body, flat head, and long tail resemble those of an otter. It is seen in red-brown and iron grey coat colours. The jaguarundi mostly hunts on the ground and also catches fish in shallow pools.

HABITAT Forest and grassland; Central and South America

LENGTH 49–83 cm (19.2–32.6 in)

STATUS Least concern

Cheetah
Acinonyx jubatus

A flexible back bone and long legs make the cheetah the fastest land animal on Earth. It stalks its prey by getting as close as possible, before sprinting to catch it.

HABITAT Grassland; Africa and Iran

LENGTH 1.2–1.45 m (4–4.7 ft)

STATUS Vulnerable

LIFE LESSONS
Cheetah cubs stay with their mother for the first 18 months, a period of rapid growth during which the cubs learn essential survival skills. The mother may catch small prey, such as a young gazelle, and leave it to her cubs to learn how to kill it.

Cheetah cubs learn to hunt by

observing
and copying

their mother's movements

Pallas's Cat

Otocolobus manul

This wild cat inhabits cold and remote mountainous regions of Asia. A long, thick coat and small ears are adaptations that ensure the Pallas's cat can survive the low temperatures and tough terrain.

HABITAT Grassland and semi-desert areas with rocky outcrops; Asia

LENGTH 46–65 cm (18–26 in)

STATUS Near threatened

The German naturalist Peter Simon Pallas first described this wild cat in 1776 and gave it a Latin name.

Leopard Cat
Prionailurus bengalensis

The most common wild cat in southern Asia is the leopard cat. They are excellent swimmers and will catch and eat frogs and crabs as well as a wide variety of other animals such as rodents, lizards, birds, and insects.

HABITAT Forest; Asia

LENGTH 45–75 cm (17.7–29.5 in)

STATUS Least concern

Leopardlike spots

Flat-headed Cat
Prionailurus planiceps

The flat-headed cat has a long, flat head and white-tipped fur, which creates a shimmering silver coat. It prefers to live by rivers and wetlands, and hunts fish but may also feed on amphibians, crustaceans, and small mammals.

Very small ears compared to most wild cats

HABITAT Wetland; Thailand, Malaysia, Sumatra, and Borneo

LENGTH 45–52 cm (17.7–20.4 in)

STATUS Endangered

Fishing Cat
Prionailurus viverrinus

As its name suggests, the fishing cat enjoys an aquatic lifestyle. It dives into water and uses its webbed paws to swim. Prey includes fish and snakes from rivers and mangrove swamps.

HABITAT
Wetland;
Asia

LENGTH
57–115 cm
(22–43 in)

STATUS
Vulnerable

Black-footed Cat
Felis nigripes

While it may be the smallest of the African wild cats, this feline is a fierce hunter. It feeds mainly on rodents and birds but also hunts reptiles and shrews. The black-footed cat is named after the black soles of its feet.

HABITAT Grassland and semi-arid regions; southern Africa

LENGTH 36–52 cm (14–20.4 in)

STATUS Vulnerable

Jungle Cat
Felis chaus

This cat has a misleading name because it lives mainly in grasslands and marshes. Jungle cats are active at night, but also at dawn and dusk.

HABITAT Wetland and grassland; Central and Southeast Asia

LENGTH 61–85 cm (24–34 in)

STATUS Least concern

Sand Cat
Felis margarita

This cat is hardly ever seen because it is nocturnal (active at night), especially in the summer. It sleeps in underground burrows on hot days, but in the summer it may rest under scrub vegetation. Although water is scarce in its habitat, the sand cat gets all the moisture it needs from what it eats.

HABITAT	Desert; Africa and Asia
LENGTH	39–52 cm (15.3–20.4 in)
STATUS	Least concern

European Wildcat
Felis silvestris

This cat looks just like a large, domestic tabby cat, but it is well capable of surviving in the wild. In mainland Europe, it feeds mainly on mice and voles, but in Scotland, rabbits and hares are its main prey.

HABITAT Woodland and scrubland; Europe

LENGTH 47–66 cm (19–26 in)

STATUS Least concern

This cat avoids human contact and is not found in urban or intensively farmed areas.

African Wildcat
Felis lybica

The North African sub-species of this wildcat is the ancestor of all domestic cats. Having been tolerated because they were good pest controllers, these cats were later taken into people's homes.

HABITAT Desert, savanna, grassland, and forest; Africa and Asia

LENGTH 41–67 cm (16–26.3 in)

STATUS Least concern

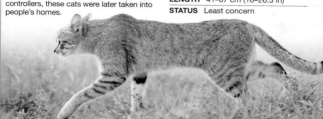

Chinese Mountain Cat
Felis bieti

The sandy yellow-orange striped coat of the Chinese mountain cat is unusual in wild cats. This small, stocky species is active from dusk to dawn, when it hunts rodents and birds.

HABITAT
High steppe grassland; China

LENGTH
68.5–84 cm (25.3–33 in)

STATUS Vulnerable

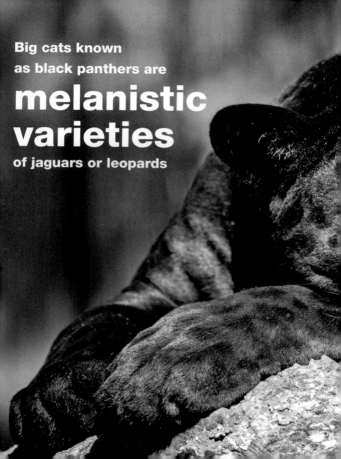

Big cats known
as black panthers are

melanistic
varieties

of jaguars or leopards

PATTERNED PANTHER
Black panthers prove that looks can be deceiving. From afar, they appear to have entirely black coats. However, up close, a pattern of rosettes or spots becomes clear. These big cats are really jaguars or leopards with the condition melanism, which makes fur and skin look darker than they are.

FOCUS ON...
PATTERNS

Wild cats have a variety of coat patterns to provide camouflage while hunting in their natural habitats.

▲ Dark rosettes on a lighter coloured coat are characteristic of both jaguars and leopards.

▲ Black stripes across orange fur help the tiger lie low in dense undergrowth.

▲ The sandy coat of a lion lets it blend into its grassland habitat when hunting prey.

Big Cats

The world's most famous felines are the big cats. These powerful predators occupy large territories and hunt down prey to survive in the wild. Most big cats roar, but exceptions include the snow leopard and the clouded leopard.

Jaguar
Panthera onca

The only big cat native to Central and South America is the jaguar. These solitary hunters kill large prey on land and also stalk turtles and caimans near water. They mark their territory with their waste or by clawing trees.

HABITAT Forest and marshland; Central and South America

LENGTH 1.2–1.7 m (4–5.5 ft)

STATUS Near threatened

Strong, stocky limbs are used to climb and swim

Lion
Panthera leo

The mighty lion is known as the "king of the jungle", although most lions live on the grassy plains of Africa. The maned males guard the territory, while the females hunt together as a team. Lions are the only big cats to live in groups, called prides.

HABITAT Forest, scrub, grassland, and desert; Africa and northwestern India

LENGTH 1.6–2.5 m (5–8.2 ft)

STATUS Vulnerable

A lion's roar can be heard from as far as 8 km (5 miles) away.

Amur Tiger
Panthera tigris altaica

The Amur tiger is the largest, heaviest, and most powerful of the big cats. These cats live in forested areas where temperatures can drop to -34°C (-29.2°F) during the winter months. They are solitary hunters but can kill large mammals, such as deer. As these tigers are found in the Siberian region of Russia, they are also called Siberian tigers.

HABITAT Forest; eastern Russia, northern China, Korean peninsula

LENGTH 1.5–2.9 m (4.7–9.5 ft)

STATUS Endangered

Bengal Tiger
Panthera tigris tigris

Dark stripes are perfect camouflage for Bengal tigers in South Asia's hot forests and grasslands. These powerful hunters use their massive paws to take down prey and use their large canine teeth to bite into its flesh.

HABITAT Indian subcontinent

LENGTH 1.5–2.9 m (4.7–9.5 ft)

STATUS Endangered

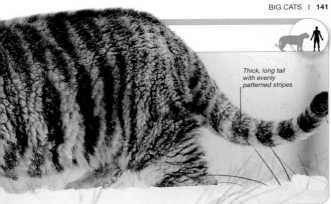

Thick, long tail with evenly patterned stripes

Leopard

Panthera pardus

This spotted, solitary big cat is an expert hunter and strong climber. Leopards can scale trees while carrying heavy prey in order to prevent other predators from stealing it.

Retractable claws used to trap prey and climb trees

HABITAT	Forest, desert, grassland, mountain, and savanna; Africa and Asia
LENGTH	0.9–1.9 m (3–6.2 ft)
STATUS	Vulnerable

Snow Leopard
Panthera uncia

The solitary snow leopard lives in remote mountainous areas. Its long, woolly fur and a thick tail that doubles up as a blanket help to provide warmth in the biting cold. This powerhouse cat can take down prey three times its weight, and often hunts large wild sheep and goats.

HABITAT	Mountain; Central Asia
LENGTH	86–125 cm (34–49 in)
STATUS	Vulnerable

Pale fur coat blends into the rocks and snow on the mountains, providing camouflage

A snow leopard can cover a distance up to six times its own body length in a single jump.

Large, padded paws keep the cat from sinking into the snow

Sunda Clouded Leopard

Neofelis diardi

The Sunda clouded leopard is named after the cloudlike pattern of its coat. It hunts on the ground for wild pigs and deer but is also an expert climber, well able to move around in trees and catch monkeys.

HABITAT	Rainforest; Southeast Asia
LENGTH	67–107 cm (26–42 in)
STATUS	Vulnerable

Snow leopards can
survive temperatures as low as
-40°C (-40°F)

SNOW SURVIVOR

The mountain ranges of Asia are home to the snow leopard. This big cat braves ferocious winds and snow storms at high altitudes of up to 6,000 m (19,685 ft). Its long fur, which thickens in the winter, provides warmth, while its huge tail can wrap around its body on cold nights.

Fascinating facts

PHYSICAL FEATURES

- Cats can **hear very high-pitched sounds** that are inaudible to human ears. Felines have a hearing range that runs from **45 to 65,000 Hz**. In contrast, human hearing ranges from 64 to 23,000 Hz.

- A **cat's heart** beats much faster than a human heart. It has a rate of **140–220 beats per minute**, compared to 60–100 beats per minute in a human.

- A cat sometimes **presses down with its front paws**. This is called **kneading**, and some experts believe it reminds a cat of when it was a kitten and would have to press its mother's tummy to get the milk flowing.

- Cats **sweat** mainly through the **pads of their four paws**. To cool down, cats also **lick themselves** and cover their fur with saliva. When the saliva evaporates, it cools the body down.

- Cats have **three eyelids** – the upper and lower lids cover the third eyelid, also called the **nictitating membrane**. It protects the eye and keeps it moist.

Like a human fingerprint, a cat's nose has its own pattern that is entirely unique.

AMAZING ABILITIES

- Cats are the only animals that **do not have the gene** that helps **taste sweetness**. So they have no interest in sweet, sugary foods. However, they can taste and enjoy fatty foods.

- Kittens **meow** when **communicating with their mothers**, but stop doing so as they mature. Adult domestic cats **meow** only to **communicate with humans** and, like kittens, do so only to get attention.

- A cat often makes a **purring sound**, which can also be felt as vibrations through its body. A happy and content cat can purr at **20–30 vibrations per second**. Kittens start purring when they are only two days old.

- Cats can **easily climb up** trees, propelled by their strong hind legs. When going up, a cat can use its **claws** to grip the tree, but when coming down, the claws do not work nearly as well.

- Cats often **rub their heads** against people they like and trust. They do so as a sign of affection as well as to **leave their own scent** on their favourite humans.

MYTHS AND LEGENDS

• In Native American folklore, **the Wampus Cat** is a shape-shifting creature, similar to the cougar, with yellow eyes, high speed, and magical powers.

• In Maya mythology, there are many **jaguar gods** – the Maya built temples to honour and worship them.

• The Olmec had myths about **werejaguars**, supernatural creatures that could shape-shift from humans to jaguars.

• Traditional stone **lion statues** have adorned buildings across China for centuries. They are thought to represent lions that would be given as gifts to royalty.

The Celts of Scotland feared the Cat Sith, or Fairy Cat – a huge, ghostly black cat with a white spot on its chest.

• The **Yule Cat**, or **Jólakötturinn**, is a giant Christmas cat in Icelandic folklore. On Christmas night, the Jólakötturinn looks in through windows to see if a child is wearing new clothes – as children who have done their chores will have new clothes as a gift. If they don't have them, it means they have not done their chores, so, as punishment, the cat eats their dinner, and in some stories, the child as well!

• The **Bakeneko** is one of many Japanese cat myths. The Bakeneko is a house cat that develops supernatural shape-shifting powers with age. It walks on its back legs, grows to the size of a human, and disguises itself as other cats or people. It causes misfortune for its owners.

RECORD BREAKERS

• The longest domestic cat living is a male Maine Coon named **Barivel**, from Italy, that measured a staggering 1.2 m (3.9 ft) in 2018.

• The smallest domestic cat on record was a male Himalayan-Persian named **Tinker toy**, from the USA, that measured 7 cm (2.75 in) from its feet to its shoulders.

• The loudest purr by a domestic cat on record registered 67.8 decibels, about the same level as the sound of a vacuum cleaner. This purr came from a cat named **Merlin** in Devon, UK, in 2015.

• The longest tail on a domestic cat on record was 44.66 cm (17.58 in), in 2018, and belongs to a silver Maine Coon named **Cygnus** in the USA.

• The wealthiest feline on record was an American mixed breed cat known as **Grumpy Cat**. It became very popular on social media and earned around US$100 million.

Cats in culture

IN HISTORY

• US President Abraham Lincoln kept cats as pets in the White House. One lucky feline named **Tabby** was once fed with a gold fork at a presidential dinner!

• **Mike the cat** helped keep pigeons away from the main gate of the British Museum in London from 1909 to 1929. The news of his passing, in 1929, was published in leading newspapers.

• A cat nicknamed **Unsinkable Sam** is said to have survived the sinking of three battleships in World War II. He first belonged to a crew member on the German battleship *Bismarck*.

• For centuries, **cats** were carried **on board ships** to control rodents on the vessels and bring good luck for the journey. But in 1975, the British Royal Navy banned cats from its ships in case they passed diseases to the crew.

• A cat named **Stubbs** was made mayor of Talkeetna, Alaska, USA in 1998. Tourists flocked to meet the mayoral feline who drank water mixed with catnip from a glass!

In the 9th century CE, an Irish monk wrote a poem called *Pangúr Bán* about his white cat.

IN BOOKS AND COMICS

• Two wild cats feature in *The Jungle Book* by the British author Rudyard Kipling. **Bagheera**, a black panther, is a loyal friend and mentor to the human boy Mowgli, while Bengal tiger **Shere Khan** is a dangerous predator.

• In 1939, the British poet T S Eliot published a **poetry collection** titled *Old Possum's Book of Practical Cats*. It was later turned into *Cats*, one of the longest-running musicals of all time.

• **Aslan the lion** features in the British author C S Lewis's book series, *The Chronicles of Narnia*. This wise lion represents all that is good in the world of Narnia.

• Published in 1957, *The Cat in the Hat* by the US author Theodor Geisel (under the name Dr Seuss) tells the tale of **a talking cat** who took two bored children on a string of amazing adventures.

• A comic strip created by the US cartoonist Jim Davis in the 1970s featured **Garfield**, a ginger cat who lived with Jon, his owner, and a dog, Odie. Garfield's love of laziness and lasagne won him fans all over the world.

IN FILM AND TV

• Captain Marvel's furry sidekick in her intergalactic battles was an orange tabby cat named **Goose**. Four different cats played Goose in the film *Captain Marvel*.

• The swashbuckling star of the *Shrek* series was based on the original fairy tale *Puss in Boots*. **Puss** was voiced by the Spanish actor Antonio Banderas in the 2011 animated film of the same name.

• **Mr Tinkles** in the 2001 film *Cats and Dogs* portrayed an evil dog-hating feline determined to take over the world.

• The iconic roaring lion logo of MGM Pictures features **Leo the lion**. Seven different lions have been used for the logo since 1924.

• The 1964 film *Born Free* tracked the life of an orphaned lioness cub named **Elsa**, who was raised in Kenya by wildlife conservationist George Adamson and his wife Joy, an artist and naturalist.

• Audiences fell in love with **Bob**, a stray ginger cat in the 2016 film *A Streetcat named Bob*. Based on a memoir by James Bowen, the film tells the story of how Bob transformed the life of James when he was homeless.

• *Two Brothers* tells the story of sibling tigers, named **Kumal** and **Sangha**, who are separated as cubs in Cambodia, and later reunited in challenging times.

• The classic American cartoon *Tom and Jerry* centres on **Tom**, a house cat, hellbent on catching little Jerry, a mouse. The antics of this comical duo have been enjoyed by audiences for decades.

• Disney's *The Lion King* features the lion cub **Simba**, whose father Mufasa is killed by his uncle Scar. Simba grows up far from home and later returns to overthrow Scar and take his place as the leader of his pride.

The Pink Panther animated series features a cartoon cat who is chased by a clumsy detective.

• A delightful character in the *Winnie-the-Pooh* stories by A A Milne was **Tigger the tiger**. He bounced around the Hundred Acre Wood with endless enthusiasm, exhausting his woodland friends along the way.

• **Sylvester**, the black and white cat, causes mischief and mayhem in the award-winning *Looney Tunes* cartoon series. He is forever chasing the yellow canary Tweetie Pie or the super-fast mouse Speedy Gonzales.

• **Salem** the cat was Sabrina's companion in the TV series *Sabrina The Teenage Witch*.

Glossary

Antibody A protein in blood that fights bacteria or other bodily threats as part of the immune system.

Awn hair The bristly hair of the undercoat.

Bicolour A coat with patches of white and one other colour.

Breed A group of cats with a distinctive appearance developed and maintained by selective breeding.

Camouflage A colour or pattern of fur that helps a wild cat blend into its natural habitat.

Carnassials Specialized cheek teeth of carnivores used to cut through flesh and bone.

Carnivore A member of Carnivora, an order (a level of biological classification); also an animal that eats meat.

Catnip A type of strong-smelling plant that releases a scented oil that is attractive to most cats.

Climate The average weather conditions in a wide area over a long period of time.

Cloning Production of an organism that is an exact genetic copy of another.

Colourpoint A coat pattern in which cats have a pale body with a darker face, ears, tail, and legs.

Crossbreed The offspring produced by crossing one cat breed with another.

Crustacean An organism with two pairs of antennae and a tough outer shell.

DNA Short for Deoxyribonucleic acid (DNA), a complex chemical molecule in a cell that carries genetic information.

Domestic cat Any feline that lives with or is cared for by humans.

Down hair Short, soft, fine hairs that form the undercoat and help keep cats warm.

Endangered species A species that is at very high risk of becoming extinct in the wild.

Family A level of biological classification; see Felidae.

Fawn A warm, pale brown colour.

Felidae The collective name for the 41 species that make up the cat family.

Felinae One of the two groups in the family Felidae, consisting of small cats, including both wild cats and the domestic cat.

Feline A cat or another animal described as being catlike; also a member of the cat family.

Feral A domestic cat that lives as a wild cat with little or no human contact.

Flehmen response A behaviour that enhances a smell by curling the upper lip upwards, forcing air past a sense organ in the mouth.

Gene The basic unit of inheritance found at a specific place on a DNA molecule and having a specific function.

Genetics The study of genes, their variation, and inheritance.

Guard hair Longer hair in the topcoat that protects the undercoat.

Habitat The natural environment of an animal or plant.

Heterochromia An eye condition in which animals have irises with two different colours.

Hock A joint in the hindleg equivalent to the human ankle and heel.

Hybrid The offspring of a cross between two different species.

Keratin A protein found in claws and hair.

Litter A group of kittens born at the same time to the same mother.

Mackerel tabby Coat pattern of narrow, black stripes on a lighter coloured coat.

Marbled pattern A classic tabby pattern in which the dark markings are more swirled and dramatic.

Melanism An inherited condition in which excessive dark pigment is produced, making the animal appear black.

Mitted coat A coat in a cat with white paws.

Mummify To preserve dead bodies by embalming them and wrapping them in cloth; a practice in ancient Egypt.

Mutation A random change in DNA that can be neutral, beneficial, or harmful.

Nocturnal A behaviour in which an animal is active at night.

Non-pedigree A cat that does not belong to any recognized breed.

Pantherinae One of the two groups in the family Felidae, consisting of 7 species of big cats.

Papillae In cats, small spoon-shaped barbs on the tongue.

Particolour Two or more clearly different colours in a cat's coat.

Pedigree A pure-bred cat of known ancestry that has specific characteristics.

Pigmentation The natural colouring of skin, fur, or hair.

Pointed pattern *see* colourpoint.

Predator A carnivorous animal that hunts down other animals to eat.

Prey An animal that is hunted and killed by another animal for food.

Retractable claws In Felidae, claws that can be drawn back into sheaths, which helps them keep sharp. Cheetahs lack sheaths.

Rex Any genetic mutation in cats that results in a curly coat.

Rosette pattern A patterned coat in which darker roselike markings provide camouflage for some wild cats.

Scent marking A behavior that conveys information to other cats. Cats spray urine, deposit droppings, and use scent glands on their bodies by rubbing against or scratching things to mark territory.

Scruff The loose, less-sensitive skin at the back of the neck of some animals.

Self: Also called solid, a cat coat consisting of only one colour.

Shaded coat A coat in which hairs are darker coloured for a quarter of their length from the tip.

Smoked coat A coat in which hairs are darker coloured for half of their length from the tip.

Tabby A coat pattern with 4 types: classic whorls, mackerel, spotted, and ticked.

Tabby-tortie A tortie cat with tabby markings.

Tapetum lucidum A layer of cells at the back of the eyes in some animals. It reflects light, helping animals to see in dim light.

Ticked coat Also called agouti – a coat in which the hairs have alternating bands of colour.

Tipped coat A coat in which hairs are darker coloured for one-eighth of their length from the tip.

Topcoat The outer layer of a cat's coat that consists of guard hairs.

Tortie Short for tortoiseshell, a coat pattern of intermingled or patchy black, red, and cream hairs, or lighter blue, lilac, or fawn, with cream hairs.

Tortie and white Called calico in the USA – tortie cat with sizeable white patches.

Tylotrichs Longer hairs found in a cat's coat that carry sensory data to the brain.

Undercoat The soft, thick, insulating hair beneath the longer protective topcoat.

Vertebra One of the bones making up the spinal column, through which the spinal cord runs.

Whiskers Stiff, mobile sensory hairs on a cat's head, throat, and forelegs, used for navigation.

White spotting White spots on a cat's coat caused by a gene that prevents production of coloured fur.

Index

Acknowledgments

Dorling Kindersley would like to thank: Bharti Bedi, Upamanyu Das, Sukriti Kapoor, Bipasha Roy, and Sai Prasanna for editorial assistance; Noopur Dalal and Baibhav Parida for design assistance; Nimesh Agrawal and Geetika Bhandari for picture research; Harish Aggarwal, Emma Dawson, Priyanka Sharma, and Saloni Talwar for the jacket; Elizabeth Wise for indexing; and Caroline Stamps for proofreading.

The publisher would like to thank the following for their kind permission to reproduce their photographs:

(Key: a-above; b-below/bottom; c-centre; f-far; l-left; r-right; t-top; column:row on cover)

123RF.com: Ana Vasileva / ABV 138cb, Eric Isselee / isselee 13crb, Aleksei Kurguzov 18c, petestock 133crb, vvvita 51crb; **Alamy Stock Photo:** Arco / G. Lacz 33ca, 122–123, Idamini 80–81, mauritius images GmbH 64–65; **Gromova Anna:** Photographer : Sergei Lubov, owner of the cat Gromova Anna 59b; **Dorling Kindersley:** The Natural History Museum, London 5ca, 7cra, Tracy Morgan Animal Photography / Jan Bradley 11cra, 39br, Tracy Morgan Animal Photography / Pat Cherry 66cla, Tracy Morgan Animal Photography / Susan Ketcher 10bc, 13crb (Hairless), University of Pennsylvania Museum of Archaeology and Anthropology 22l, Jerry Young 131ca; **Dreamstime.com:** Annestaub 57, Appfind 138cla, Nilanjan Bhattacharya 5cb, Chris De Blank 85cb, Lukas Blazek 7crb, 107tl, 121, Bulltus Casso 9c, Feng Cheng 113b, Chavdar Chernev 87, Colicaranica 20–21, Brett Critchley 113cla, Dbeatson 124crb, Dirkr 17tl, Judith Dzierzawa 39ca, Eastmanphoto 124clb, Ecophoto 6clb, Elgreko74 7cb, Ewastudio 34crb, Farinoza 107tc, Boyce Fitzgerald 28, Jaroslav Frank 136–137, Christopher Freeman 16crb, Eugeniu Frimu 97clb, Claire Fulton 132–133c, Astrid Gast 96, Gator 111, Edwin Godinho 134, Jeff Grabert 6crb, 119, Hedrus 18b, Nynke Van Holten 12crb, 37crb, 52br, Christian Hornung 77crb, Idenviktor 35, Eric Isselée / Isselee 91cla, Isselee 10br, 25cr, 38b, 73b, 78ca, 85ca, 105lb, Jhaviv 126, Vladislav Jirousek 130, Dmitry Kalinovsky 68clb, Anna Krivitskaia 32clb, 78b, Inna Kyselova 53, Susan Leggett 11cr, Oleg Liashenko 26, Linncurrie 72, 97crb, Maggymeyer 139, Mikael Males 19cl, 124ca, Ievgeniia Miroshnichenko 79, Nousha 82, Alexander Oganezov 2–3c, Onetouchspark 105br, Pavelmidi1968 127cla, Petr Jilek / Pitrs10 86cra, Arsenii Popel 14–15, Stu Porter 115, Dmitri Pravdjukov 61, 103cb, Denys Prokofyev 30–31, Ondřej Prosický 135ca, 140–141tl, Rgbe 127cb, Karen Richards 5crb, Arun Roisri 131b, Sandyprints 43crb, Sarahthexton 38cla, Scheriton 143, Kucher Serhii 39clb, 40cla, Sikth 70b, Dennis Donohue / Silksatsunrise 112, Elizaveta Smirnova 100–101, Svand 7clb, Pavel Sytsko 41, Taniawild 106clb, Sergey Taran 60cra, 106–107b, 108–109, Sarayut Thaneerat 138cl, Tomonishi 110, Katrina Trninich 83clb, Wing Ho Tsang 31cla, Nikolai Tsvetkov 60clb, Lillian Tveit 125, Pavlo Vakhrushev 104, Vladyslav Starozhylov / Vladstar 32crb, Sina Vodjani 22r, Volodymyrkrasyuk 141crb, Anthony Woodhouse 24cr, Lianquan Yu 135crb, Zafi123 6c, Abeselom Zerit 142, 144–145; **Fotolia:** Anatolii 8–9b, Eric Isselee 9cr; **Getty Images:** C.O.T / a.collectionRF 46–47, Corbis / Fabio Petroni 45, Universal Images Group / Auscape 88–89; **iStockphoto.com:** GomezDavid 116–117, Jolkesky 54–55; **Shutterstock:** Sergey Ginak 74–75; **SuperStock:** Juniors 66b, Minden Pictures 128–129

Cover images: *Front:* **Dorling Kindersley:** Tracy Morgan Animal Photography / Susan Ketcher (6:2); **Dreamstime.com:** Isselee (2:5), Dmitri Pravdjukov (9:2), Kucher Serhii (7:2), Sergey Taran (4:1), Nikolai Tsvetkov (2:1), Volodymyrkrasyuk (8:1); **Getty Images:** EyeEm / Steven Heap br; *Spine:* **Getty Images:** EyeEm / Steven Heap

All other images © Dorling Kindersley

For further information see: **www.dkimages.com**